KICK BUTT
HIRING
HANDBOOK

KICK BUTT
HIRING
HANDBOOK

HOW TO FIND THE RIGHT EMPLOYEES, RIGHT NOW

AMY J WOLF

Prosper Publishing

Lodi, CA

Published by:

Prosper Publishing LLC

Paperback: 978-0-9986942-0-7

Mobi: 978-0-9986942-1-4

Epub: 978-0-9986942-2-1

Library of Congress Cataloging Number: 2017937841

Library of Congress data on file with the publisher

Printed in the United States of America

10 9 8 7 6 5 4 3 2 1

CONTENTS

INTRODUCTION

Wednesday afternoon, 2:00 p.m.

Candice: "Hello, this is Candice with ABC Logistics. I'm calling regarding the resume you submitted to our company for the opening as a daytime data-entry specialist. We would like to bring you in for an interview at your earliest convenience."

Applicant: (*in a gloomy monotone*) "Uh, let's see, okay. I just woke up. Let me find something to write on."

Candice: "No problem, let me know when you are ready."

Applicant: "Ugh (*yelling*) Kids! Shut up! I'm on the phone! (*muttering*) Stupid kids never stop fighting. (*sighs*) Okay, I guess I'm ready."

Candice: "Are you able to come in this afternoon?"

Applicant: "Weelll, I'm in the middle of a nap, and then I had some other things to do. Probably not today."

Candice: "Sure, okay, let's look at tomorrow. How does that work for you? We are available anytime between eight a.m. and six p.m."

Applicant: "Honestly, I don't usually get up that early. I am not a morning person. Really evening is better cuz I will have someone to watch my kids then anyway. I don't have anyone to watch them during the day. Can we do it after six?"

Candice: (*hesitantly*) "Well, those are the hours that we're at the office. Can you make arrangements to get here during our business hours?"

Applicant: (*irritated*) "All right, whatever, I will see what I can do. Let's try to do it tomorrow as late as possible."

Candice: "Sure, we will schedule it for five p.m., that's as late as we can start and still have time to conduct the interview."

Applicant: "All right, thanks. Bye."

Candice: "Wait— You may need the address and phone number. That would probably be helpful."

Applicant: "Oh, yeah, okay."

Candice: "We're at 1234 Broadway, Suite 102. When you get here, the door marked Employees Only will be locked. Go ahead and knock, and you will be buzzed in. If you have any questions, you can call me back at (999) 555-1234."

Applicant: "How do I get there?"

Candice: "Are you able to Google Map the address, or use a GPS?"

Applicant: "I don't really use computers much. Can you just tell me how to get there?"

Anyone who has conducted their share of job interviews knows this sinking feeling: You call an applicant to set up an interview, and within seconds, you know the person on the end of the line is not a good fit for the job. Candice is staffing a day-shift opening for computer-intensive work. In a minute-long phone call, she has already learned that this applicant does not like working on computers, is not a morning person, and would need someone to watch her children during the shift in question.

Our applicant also does not ask questions to make sure to obtain all the information she needs before she even shows up for the interview. Candice has already committed to a meeting with the applicant. Should she cancel, or go through with the interview and waste precious time interviewing someone she already knows won't be a good fit?

My husband and I encountered this challenge and many more when we started our first business, a medical billing company, nearly fifteen years ago. We spent weeks setting up interviews and meeting applicants, many of whom seemed like poor fits right away. Before long, we opened a second business, a nonemergency medical transport company. This business grew so rapidly that we frequently needed to hire two to three new employees at a time, sometimes adding staff every few weeks.

Today, we have two companies and over thirty employees in two areas of business near Sacramento, California.

Our rapid growth made the routine of mismatched applicants and fruitless interviews even more frustrating. Before long, we took a hard look at our interview process and found ways to streamline and improve it—because we simply couldn't afford to spend so much time on staffing. There's nothing like working under pressure to achieve results.

We took our interview process, which was decent but not perfect, and turned it into the amazingly efficient and successful system I now share with you. Our staffing system has simplified our lives immensely, and it can do the same for your small, growing entrepreneurial business. And maybe even help those of you in larger companies.

In addition to breaking down our system into an easy-to-follow process for each stage of hiring, I'll also discuss some of the methods we've tried in the past and what we liked and didn't like about each.

Along the way, I'll relate some stories about the good, bad, and ugly moments in conducting job interviews. Anyone with extensive hiring experience has a collection of funny stories, and I'll share the best of mine with you. Here's the first one.

DRUNK DRIVING

An older gentleman applied for a driver opening with our transport company. Because of the nature of the work, we thoroughly scrub our applicants to make sure they are a good, safe fit. In our want ads, we always state explicitly that a background check and drug/alcohol screening are required.

I set up an initial phone interview with the man who seemed promising. He was quite the social butterfly, was very involved in politics, worked with the community, and recently retired from a career as a parole agent. He was looking for a part-time job to supplement his retirement income and meet people. I was not convinced, based on his background, that he was an amazing fit for the job, but I loved his attitude and motivation. At the least, I genuinely thought our passengers would enjoy his company. He was friendly and a little quirky.

As long as he passed all the screenings, I thought he just might work out. We have had multiple retired folks work for us, and they have all been wonderful. So I gave him all the necessary paperwork for the screenings and asked him to keep me updated on his progress completing them.

After a week, I had heard nothing. So I asked my business partner/husband to touch base. He left repeated messages for the applicant, but still nothing. Finally we received a call from the drug/alcohol screening firm. They informed us the applicant had called three times to set up a time for a screening, and three times rescheduled or simply failed to show up. My husband kept calling the missing applicant.

Finally, the man answered, drunk. Not just tipsy, but really hammered, at noon. This explained why he had repeatedly rescheduled his drug and alcohol screening. Needless to say, he was not hired. Just one example of the many reasons to make sure you are thoroughly screening your applicants.

1

HELP WANTED—THE HUNT IS ON

Posting a job ad might seem like a simple first step. But the wording you choose for your ad can make the difference between a batch of appropriate candidates and mismatched applicants who will only waste your valuable time.

The best ad is detailed enough to express your needs, but not so long that it scares off potential applicants. You should begin by positioning your company as a highly desirable employer. Strong openings look like this: "*The premier marketing company in the area is looking for a new sales team member,*" or "*The fastest-growing service provider in the area is seeking a driver.*" Right off the bat, your company comes across as successful, important, and appealing.

Next, your ad copy should clearly define the traits that are important to you, based on the job opening. Before you write the copy, make a list of attributes, rank them by priority, and incorporate the top dozen or so traits into your ad. If I am looking for a customer service rep, someone who has to be on the phone all day and type up messages, my ad would include a description like this:

If you're the Customer Service Rep we are looking for, you love to smile, focus on helping customers, and enjoy talking on the phone. You are friendly, pleasant, organized, and detail oriented. You'll be patient, conscientious, and considerate as you assist our clients with their accounts. You'll also be described as positive, personable, and mature—a relaxed team player with high standards.

You will want to conclude your ad with any necessary qualifications. This would include any skills a successful applicant will need such as level of education, driver's license, typing speed, and certifications. Including explicit qualification requirements should lower the number of unsuitable resumes that wind up on your desk (or your Inbox with online applicants).

Should your ad mention a starting wage? It depends. If you are hiring for an entry-level position with no wiggle room on pay, yes, it is helpful to list the wage. Otherwise you might receive applicants who are looking for a wage higher than you can offer, which leads to wasted time for both parties. However, if you are willing to negotiate on the starting wage for the position based on experience, you may want to leave specific wage information out. If you list a wage on the low side, you may deter more experienced applicants. I will touch on this in the face-to-face interview section.

Once you have written your ad, your next decision is where to post it. Finding the solution for your firm will take a bit of trial and error, as it depends on your location and the type of employees you are seeking.

In the past, we have had modest success using Craigslist, a popular classified ad network. In our region in California, Craigslist charges $15 to post an ad. This rate is reasonable, but it can get expensive if you are frequently posting job openings.

The benefit of Craigslist is that the people who respond to ads there are typically active job seekers, as opposed to those who cruise job search engines and listing sites, such as Indeed.com or Monster, where job hunters can submit their resume simply by clicking a button.

Because responding to a Craigslist posting requires a little more effort, your responders tend to be more serious about the job. The disadvantage of Craigslist is the potential cost for posting, as well as limits on how many regional Craigslist sites you can post an ad in.

When we need a bigger applicant pool, we use Indeed.com. An ad that would elicit thirty to fifty applicants on Craigslist might result in as many 700 applicants via Indeed. There is no need to pay to "boost" the post. I always use Indeed's free option, and believe me, it gets plenty of applicants. Job posting websites generate tons of applicants; this is both a pro and a con.

Now you have a huge pile of resumes to sift through. Some of those applicants didn't read the fine print on your thoughtfully worded listing and just fire off a resume with a few clicks. They may not have the necessary skills, nor are they even interested in the type of job you advertised. They automatically submit their resume to any opening in their area and hope for a phone call. Upon talking to this type of applicant, you may find they were never interested in your job.

However, sites like Indeed do offer this advantage: a search tool for sorting through resumes, even if the applicant did not apply for your position. You can set parameters for a search, find people whose resumes fit the specifications, and send them an interview invite.

If you prefer hunting for candidates who match your preferences rather than collecting applications based on a want ad, LinkedIn is another helpful tool for finding skilled people in your region.

2

PROCESSING THE RESUME PILE LIKE A PRO—YES OR NO

Now that you have hundreds of applicants from your Indeed ad or your other sources, let's figure out which candidates you want to interview. Obviously you don't have the time to bring in hundreds of possible hires, nor would you want to do all that work. What you're looking for in resumes will hinge on the job you are hiring for, so quickly scan your applications for possible hires with the necessary skills.

When I filter through resumes, I mentally create three piles: NO, YES, and MAYBE. The resumes are usually submitted in some online format, so I only print out my YES and MAYBE resumes. I won't need to go back to my NO pile anyhow. I don't always dip into my MAYBE stack, but it's nice to have in reserve, in case no one in the YES pile blows me away.

Quickly skim for typos. Keep in mind how lazy someone must be if they can't be bothered to run spell-check. You might consider overlooking small errors, like a missing capital letter or an extra space, that an automatic spell-check can miss. However, if you find more than one grammatical error in a cover letter, especially if this position will handle any sort of correspondence, consider that a red flag. On the opposite side of the coin, if you are looking for someone to do manual labor, a few typos may not be a concern.

Indeed provides resume templates, and some applicants will completely skip over portions, leaving blanks like [Enter job dates here] or [Employer Name]. This can be a warning sign of a careless attitude. If a job applicant won't take an extra couple minutes to review their resume to make sure they filled in every box, what quality of work will they produce at your company? If high standards and accuracy are important to you, consider these for the NO stack.

For previous generations, working at the same company for decades at a time was typical, and generally seen as a positive trait on a resume. It showed commitment, dedication, and loyalty. However, the average job today lasts two to five years. Changing employers and careers is much more common and has its own benefits. Well-traveled employees can bring in fresh ideas and new perspectives. Don't let the length of time someone works for a company deter you, but keep an eye on a few relevant considerations.

Take a look at the time frame between an applicant's jobs. Does it seem like they are leaving one job without having the next one lined up? There are often good reasons for this, like taking care of family, or an illness, but frequently hopping from job to job without a back-up plan is a red flag.

Is the applicant getting fired from jobs due to poor performance? Are they unreliable or irresponsible? Unless you see something really interesting or promising on a resume with lots of unexplained hiccups, it should probably go in the NO stack. If you see something that really interests you on one of these resumes, consider putting it in the MAYBE stack.

What about references? While you may not require references on a resume, it is always nice when they are included. Unsolicited references show that an applicant is confident in their abilities and has people who are willing to back them up. If references are not provided, and you wind up seriously considering the applicant, be sure to ask, as testimonials from former supervisors and colleagues make for valuable information later in the hiring process.

Once you complete a quick review of a resume and deem the applicant worth considering at greater length, read the actual job descriptions of their previous positions. As you read through, consider the following: How does the candidate describe their duties and skills? Are you seeing vague descriptors like "worked hard" or "showed up on time"? Or does the resume list concrete claims that can be supported?

An example of a concrete skill would be "successfully assisted 100 customers per day." Or "reliably exceeded quarterly goals set by manager for two years in a row." It's always nice to hear what the applicant feels are their strongest skills, but hard details on their performance are even better.

Finally, when evaluating a promising candidate, remember that the skills they do or don't possess aren't a guarantee of how well—or poorly—they might fit at your company. Just because an applicant has never worked in a medical billing office, for example, doesn't mean they don't have the capacity to learn that type of work. Sometimes the best employees are those without any prior experience. You can teach them the way you want the work done.

Our company uses more technology than comparably sized billing companies in our area. Therefore, someone coming from another billing firm won't know how our processes work, regardless of years in the field, because our systems vary greatly from what they're used to.

If an applicant has good typing skills, basic computer knowledge, and a desire to learn, I am always willing to teach the specifics of a position. I look for someone who seems comfortable on a computer and on the phone, and sometimes I look for education in the medical or medical administration fields.

Generally, professional courses only provide an overview, and an applicant with medical admin training will not know all that much more than any other applicant without practical work experience. But that background indicates an interest in the medical field. Many times that interest reflects a desire—and willingness—to learn.

One of our star employees came to us in her early twenties. Her only work experience was at a local department store. She attended school for medical billing, but was quite unaware of the billing process. What I remember most was her determination to learn, but there was one hurdle she had to clear: She could not type. Not at all. She could manage fifteen to twenty words a minute via hunt-and-peck.

But something told me she had the potential to be really good, so we decided to hire her on the condition that she would work on an online typing tutor for the first twenty minutes of every day, until her typing skills reached our minimum requirement. That girl blew my socks off. She reached her goal in only a couple weeks and went on to be one of the quickest and most accurate data-entry people we've ever had.

If an employee has the drive and determination to learn something, they can become a productive team member, regardless of a lack of experience. Keep that in mind when sweeping through resumes. Look for anything on a resume that may clue you in to an interest or talent that could roll over into your company's work. A good fit is not always about the skill. Sometimes a hire can succeed through ambition and determination.

WRONG COMPANY

We have had many interns/externs through our company. We complete a brief face-to-face interview, to give them the experience as well as to ensure they will be a good fit. If the interview goes well, we begin their training immediately following.

One day we were waiting for a new intern to report to work. A petite young girl in scrubs walked through our door. Many of the schools require the students to wear scrubs to class and for internships, so I didn't question her attire. We led her to the interview room and proceeded with the interview. She completed the questioning, and she was set up on a computer to begin working.

About an hour into the training, she asked our supervisor where the dentist worked. The supervisor looked at her quizzically and asked her what she was talking about. She stated her intern director told her she was going to be working near the dentist during her internship.

Eventually we figured out she was supposed to be across the hall, at the dental office. We led her over to the dentist's office and had to explain why his intern was late for her first day. Important lesson learned: confirm the interviewee's name before beginning.

3

CONDUCTING THE PHONE INTERVIEW—IT'S LIKE SPEED DATING

You've sorted the resumes, and worked through the YES pile to get a list of potential candidates. It's finally time to start the interview process with phone interviews. Yes, I did say "phone interviews." This is our secret to getting through thirty or more preliminary interviews in a day.

Remember at the beginning of the book when Candice called to set up an interview and was instantly sorry about committing to the applicant? One day I had a lightning-bolt idea: Why not modify the interview process, reduce the number of questions, and breeze through a ten- to fifteen-minute phone interview? Quick preliminary conversations give you a decent idea of which candidates you want to meet face-to-face.

Another bonus about the first-round phone interview: Even if the applicant is working during the day, they can easily fit a fifteen-minute phone interview into a break or lunch. If they live out of the area, a quick phone call saves them a long drive for a short interview. A fast first-round telephone interview simplifies the hiring process for all involved.

Make sure before you make the phone calls you print up a list of the questions and attach them to the resume so you will have them accessible when the applicant answers.

I'll walk you through the questions I ask during the phone interview, but first let's take a long view of the whole process.

Grab your YES pile and dig in. Call them one at a time. If they answer, ask if they have time for a fifteen-minute phone interview right then or, if they prefer, schedule the call for a more convenient time. Continue this process, calling back to back, completing interview after interview. If the applicant decides to schedule the interview, *do not* call the applicant back at the appointment time. Make it clear you expect them to call you back. If they want the job, they should be responsible for following up with you, on time.

Some applicants ask me if I can call them back, even after telling them to call me. That is instantly a mark against them. If they are truly interested in the job, they need to be driven enough to call you. If they call back late, that is another mark against them. Keep track of these little points, because they can be the tie breakers in a final decision.

If an applicant is a few minutes late calling back, make a note on their interview sheet. If they are more than five minutes late for their interview, you might choose to reject their call altogether. If they can't call in on time for a scheduled interview, how reliable will they be as an employee?

If I receive a voice-mail, I introduce myself and tell them I am calling in response to a resume submitted to us for a job opening, and I would like to conduct a fifteen-minute phone interview. I provide the applicant with my name and number and request a callback. I wait about twenty-four hours, and if no response is received, I leave one more message. If I do not receive a callback in response to the second message, I shred the resume and move on.

Once you have approval to begin the interview process, briefly run down what the interview will consist of. Tell them you'll go through a brief job history and then ask a few general questions, and that will be it for today. Explain that you are narrowing down the number of applicants to a handful that will be brought in for face-to-face interviews.

Before beginning the actual interview, you may want to tick through the job requirements. If there is a minimum age requirement, driver's license, or certifications involved, confirm the applicant read through them and fulfills all the requirements. Then you can get started with the interview.

I also intentionally avoid telling the applicant much about our company at the beginning of this process. I like to hear their unbiased answers. If a face-to-face meeting is in store, that is when I will run down the company history and job duties in a little more detail.

I start the fifteen-minute session by asking applicants about three of their previous jobs. You may choose their three most recent jobs, or if you are looking for particular skills, you may jump around their resume to ask about positions that are more pertinent to your opening. Either way is fine. For all three jobs, I ask the following questions:

1. Where and how did you find the job?
2. What were your job duties and were you promoted?
3. What was your favorite part of the job?
4. What was your least favorite part of the job?
5. When and why did you leave the job?
6. Did you give notice, and if so, how long was the notice and did you work it out?
7. Did you have another job lined up when you left?

Here's what to look for in the answers to these questions:

Question 1: Where and how did you find the job?

You'll often see a trend in the responses here. People tend to find their jobs the same way. The three most common are these: A friend or family member told them about the opening; they applied through a job search engine; or they found the work through a temp agency. Here are the pros and cons of each scenario.

Via family member/friend

Pros: This suggests the friend or family member was confident in the applicant's skills or abilities; otherwise, they wouldn't refer them for the job.

Cons: Can reflect a lazy attitude. If applicants are never finding a job for themselves, they may lack self-motivation.

Job search engine

Pros: They are actively looking for jobs, which suggests motivation.

Cons: Some job seekers use sites like Indeed lazily and apply for everything. These shotgun-approach applicants sometimes have little interest in the jobs they apply for.

Temp agency

Pros: Those with temp experience often have diverse skills picked up at various offices, and you can infer that they don't enjoy just sitting around idly when unemployed. You should ask if they were ever offered a permanent position at any of their temp employers. A permanent hire is not always a possibility, no matter how good a temp is, but this info can still tell you whether this person demonstrated value to their employer.

Cons: People who work through temp agencies often have a short-term-employee attitude. They enjoy frequent breaks in between jobs and may not want to commit to a permanent full-time position. Prod a little about why they are working through a temp agency. Is it because they are actively looking for a job and have bills to pay, or is it because they prefer temporary employment?

Question 2: What were your job duties and were you promoted?

Look for two specifics in the answer to this question. First, what skills did they develop during their employment? Did they have any duties that could easily roll over to your company's opening? Second, pay attention to whether their job duties changed at their previous gig. Were they taught new skills? Did someone higher up see potential in them?

This is a good time to ask how long they were there (if their resume didn't specify) and how much time passed between each promotion or new skill they learned. In most scenarios, if the applicant was at a job for any length of time, learning new skills and getting promoted are signs of hard work, dependability, and promise.

Question 3: What was your favorite part of the job?

This is a fun opportunity to find out what the applicant's passion is. Do they enjoy working with customers? If so, sitting behind a desk or on a production line may not be the best fit for them. Do they enjoy working on computers more than anything? If so, a job as a restaurant manager may not be a match.

It's worth remembering that some applicants may not have figured out what their niche is. Find out what the applicant's interests are, because if you place an employee in the wrong job, they will be miserable, and the quality of work will suffer. As simple as this question seems, the responses can be revealing. When you ask this question in relation to three different jobs, you may start to see a trend in their answers.

Question 4: What was your least favorite part of the job?

This is the flip side of question 3, and another chance to gauge an applicant's fit for your opening. It is not unusual for someone who worked at a restaurant or department store to list cleaning up or tidying their work area as least favorite, and that is fine. You may not get much out of this question, in some instances, but still pay attention to the answers. If someone tells you they hate working on computers, don't consider them for a desk job with a lot of computer work.

Question 5: When and why did you leave the job?

Be careful with this one: Word the question exactly how it is listed here. This phrasing is more likely to elicit honest responses, regardless of the scenario the applicant is recounting. You want to provide an opportunity for applicants to speak frankly about what led up to their departure from a job. Even if they are not completely honest about their reasons for leaving, you can sometimes get a glimpse of a disagreement with a coworker or superior—information that can guide an educated decision on how this person might fit in your work environment.

You will be surprised how many people openly tell you they were fired or let go; many will even share the reason. If they don't volunteer the reason for a departure, ask. They may or may not tell you the truth, but there is value in making your applicant squirm. Sometimes you can hear them fidgeting or formulating a nice way to phrase the truth. Whether the end result of their squirming is fact or fiction, their behavior while relaying the story is often telling. You would be amazed at what you can pick up over the phone.

Another item to note: If an applicant tells you they were laid off, *always* ask how many people were laid off in total, and how the company chose whom to release. If the person had only been with the employer for a few months, they would have been an obvious choice for a layoff. But consider the number of people let go. Was it five or fifty? If the applicant was one in fifty laid off, that speaks to an employer shedding salary regardless of the quality of the workers let go. But if only five people were laid off, why was the applicant one of the five let go? Ask more questions; it's acceptable to prod a little.

Question 6: Did you give notice, and if so, how long was the notice and did you work it out?

This is a character question. Does the applicant have upstanding morals and ethics? If they feel a responsibility to the company they worked for, they will give notice. Are they dependable? Circumstances sometimes arise that prevent even dedicated employees from providing notice, but this question is still worth asking.

Question 7: Did you have another job lined up when you left?

You can ask the candidate about any three jobs in any order. But when you choose their three most recent jobs and move in chronological order from oldest to newest, you can follow their work history through time. You may notice gaps in their job history. Ask questions about what they did during those times.

If you skip around their job history, it can be harder to identify gaps. This is the reason behind this last question. If they chose to leave a job without another one lined up, why? If there is not a clear and legitimate reason, this applicant may lack responsibility, or perhaps has not been completely honest. It is possible that the decision to leave was made for them, and they were not forthcoming in their previous answers.

HONESTY IS THE BEST POLICY

I once did a phone interview with a young lady who had listed her high school graduation date on the resume. It wasn't advanced calculus to figure out that she was fairly young (under thirty), yet she had multiple pages of job history. My plan going in was to quiz her on this job history using her past three jobs. But once I began this particular interview, I could not help myself. I was intrigued by how many jobs this young woman had held.

When I asked her why she left the first of the three previous positions, she told me she had been laid off. I asked the same question about a second job: this time, her firm had been downsizing. I got to the third job, and it turned out the company moved out of the area and let her go. Layoffs and closures are fairly common occurrences. But her responses made me even more curious about her long track record. So I asked about a few more (she had so many for me to choose from).

For the fourth job, she told me her employer had been bought by another company. I was seeing a trend: She had been laid off from every job she'd ever had, if her answers were completely honest, which frankly I was beginning to doubt. When I asked about a fifth job, her response was, "To be really honest, I got in a fight with the boss and threatened him, so they told me they didn't think I was a good fit for the job anymore." Maybe she really was laid off the other four times, because she sure seemed honest about that fifth job.

Next: General Interview Questions

After these work-history questions, you can move into the general interview, my favorite part, if only for the interesting answers that tend to pop out. For starters, if the applicant is not currently working, **ask what they have been doing since their last job**. Self-improvement, education, or volunteering are all ideal answers that signal potential.

On the contrary, "taking it easy" or something similar can be a warning sign. For how long have they been taking it easy, and why? Can they not find a job? Do they prefer to be unemployed? Are they lazy about their job search? These are not necessarily questions you will find the answer to, but are factors to consider in your final decision.

Ask what their five-year career goal is. What you are looking for in this answer depends on your needs. Are you looking for a long-term employee who will receive significant training and thus become an investment that you'll want to retain for a long time? If so, someone who is planning to attend nursing school in a year's time is not the best fit.

If an applicant says they want to move up the ranks and become a manager, but your company has five employees, all in different roles, working independently, that person may not be a good fit.

In addition, if they express interest in rising to manager or supervisor, the initial interview is your opportunity to find out how serious they are. **Ask them why they feel they are qualified**

to be a manager, what steps they will take to reach that goal, and what they have done in their personal time to work toward those steps. Their response to these questions will let you know if the applicant takes action or simply daydreams.

Another answer you'll likely hear: a career goal of "coasting into retirement." This is a common answer from people who have had a career and retired, but want to supplement their income. They express no interest in becoming a manager or in supervising other staff members. We have had multiple employees of this type, and they were infamous for coasting on the clock, playing solitaire, taking frequent coffee breaks, talking on the phone, and socializing. If they want to coast into retirement, perhaps a temp job is a better position for them.

Remember, a good hire is a fit for both the employer *and* the employee, or the new hire will not truly excel. You are not doing a job seeker a favor by hiring them for a position that won't make them happy in the long run.

Next you'll ask practical questions: **What are your desired hours?** and **What is your desired wage?** Even though ads sometimes specify hours or a wage range, people apply for so many jobs that they often do not remember the specifics. It is important to know their expectations.

When Candice set up an interview in our opening example, the applicant she called was clearly not a morning person. The phone interview gives the applicant an opportunity to share basic information with you. They may prefer mornings and getting off early, or they may prefer swing shift, or evenings and weekends.

Gauging their desired wage gives you a hint as to whether the applicant is a fit. Get a sense of their willingness to negotiate down to your ideal number. If they would like to make $18 an hour, but you were hoping to pay $15, ask more questions.

Once you have an idea of their desired wage, you can follow up. **What is the minimum you would be able to accept?** This will let you know if they are willing to negotiate. Some people have cornered themselves into a certain cost of living and have no wiggle room. It is important to find out if you can afford their desired minimum wage, so you don't waste any time on someone who needs higher-paying work.

The final piece of the phone interview is more abstract. Ask applicants to **list the top three things they want from a job**. You can give them some examples if necessary, but try to get their own personal answers rather than agreement with your suggestions. You will hear ideas like teamwork, stability, benefits, a good wage.

Beware of those who list pay as a priority, or mention only rewards they want to get out of the job, as opposed to what they might contribute. This can be a sign of a "me" mentality, and keeping "me" people happy is often difficult. They will never make enough, and the grass will always be greener on the other side. They frequently become poorly performing employees after some time, or look to switch jobs if they feel they are not being fairly compensated for their contributions. Employees like this can affect overall office morale if they are vocal about how they feel.

Some encouraging answers to this question: A positive work environment, friendly colleagues, preferred working hours, or contributing in a team environment.

Wrapping Up the Phone Interview

Once you finish your questions, close the conversation by letting them know that you are conducting interviews for a few more days, and they can call you back on a given day to find out whether they are on the call-back list for a face-to-face interview.

Now you'll make a second set of YES, NO, and MAYBE piles, based on the phone conversations. If you're toward the end of your calls and you like someone, you might schedule their face-to-face meeting right then and there. But in most scenarios, don't rush. Take a moment to review answers after the call before committing to a second interview. You can provide an assistant with the list of people on your call-back list and perhaps have the YES callers forwarded so you can personally schedule the second interview, or if you prefer, have your assistant set them up.

One more note: I usually do not schedule my MAYBE stack unless I have completed second-round interviews with all my YES people and still haven't found a fit.

OPEN MOUTH, INSERT FOOT

Sometimes you just have to let a person talk, and they will tell you all you need to know. I conducted one phone interview with a gentleman who initially came off as pleasant and friendly. He was polite, cordial, and seemingly happy to interview with me. I was feeling really optimistic, even though we were only five minutes into our conversation.

Finally, we came to his most recent job, a position at a fairly large, well-known chain of stores. He told me he had chosen to quit. I asked him to tell me more about why he left, or what he had been doing with his time since. He said he decided to take some time off to spend with his family.

Before I could ask another question, he shared more than I had bargained for. He explained he had worked for the chain for over six months. Employees at the firm received bonuses based on production. According to the applicant, he would always overproduce and qualify for his bonuses. He was the hardest worker there.

But there was a catch. If an employee took an unexcused day off, they would lose their bonus for that week. The applicant took some days off here and there to be with his kids, so he lost his bonuses. According to him, that was "bull*@#." If he worked hard, he should have gotten his bonus. Instead he was punished for spending time with his kids. He was pretty sure his employer was racist, since they had taken away his hard-earned bonuses. He was also fairly certain other employees at the firm were getting away with things that he was not because they were not a minority. The company was crooked and dishonest, and they were stealing his bonuses just because they were mean and didn't like him.

His manager had always had it out for him, from the very beginning. He was obviously the victim in the situation, and his unexcused absence from work was just an opening for them to treat him unfairly and take away the money they owed him.

This tirade went on for nearly thirty minutes. About ten minutes in, I got up and started making copies and doing things I needed to do around the office. I had him on my cordless headset, so I would say "okay" and "mmhmm, I see" every once in a while.

Needless to say, by the time our lengthy interview was complete, I placed his resume in my NO stack.

4

TIME TO FACE-TO-FACE THE FACTS

You'll want to limit your face-to-face interviews to fifteen or fewer candidates, unless you plan on hiring more than two or three people. In-person meetings are a bigger commitment, so be careful about overbooking second-round interviews. If you do not find any candidates that are your ideal fit in the first group of live interviews, you can always book another round with different applicants from the YES pile, or consider a few from your MAYBE stack.

Very often in second-round interviews, candidates who blew you away on the phone will leave you baffled, wondering what you ever saw in them. This is why meeting in person is so important. Even if the face-to-face encounter only lasts fifteen minutes, it is a necessary part of the interview process, so don't skip it.

The phrase "you can't judge a book by its cover" is relevant in face-to-face interviews. This may go against what you have been told about sizing people up. But rather than judging an applicant by their style or what they are wearing, consider whether the applicant looks like they made an effort. If they didn't bother to comb their hair or even take a shower, this could represent laziness, but don't let clothing choices, piercings, or tattoos deter you from giving an applicant a chance if they possess the necessary skills. As long as they are willing to work hard and follow any uniform guidelines or dress codes (and practice good hygiene), it doesn't matter what they wear in their off time.

When the applicant arrives, greet them, seat them, and start with some small talk. You want to make them comfortable. The more relaxed they are with you, the more they will tell you. Once they have loosened up a little, explain that you are going to conduct a different type of interview this time. Most of your questions the second time around will tell you more about the applicant's personality, how they will handle certain situations based on past responses to similar scenarios, and a little about their problem-solving skills. You are trying to find out if they are going to be confrontational or a pushover, or are simply lazy.

I usually ask the first set of questions in three parts, allowing the applicant to answer the first component before moving on to the next one. First, ask the applicant to tell you about "a specific time when…" Use a scenario that seems like it might provide interesting feedback, preferably something they might encounter in your company, then follow up by asking how they handled that situation, and finally ask them what the end result of the situation was. Sometimes, depending on the scenario, you might finish by asking what they learned from the experience.

Here are some questions we ask, and the reasons why. Keep in mind you are not limited to these questions. This section of the interview is an opportunity for you to be creative and learn about the person sitting across from you.

- **Tell me about a specific time when you dealt with an irate customer.**
  - ☐ **Tell me what action you took.**
  - ☐ **How did the situation end?**

Here we find out how the applicant handles confrontation. Do they get angry, do they try to help, do they just listen, or do they get a supervisor? Their answers will help you decide if the applicant will be a good fit for the position.

If they are able to problem-solve and handle a conflict themselves, they may have potential for a supervisory position. If they get angry, they may not be good with clients, but could still do productive work alone on a computer. If the applicant let the irate customer talk it out, they may be a good listener and possibly a fabulous customer service rep. There are not necessarily right answers to these questions; instead, people's behavior provides clues as to what positions they are suited for. You would be amazed at how people answer some of these questions.

- **Give me an instance when you didn't think you were going to make a deadline.**
  - ☐ **What steps did you take to meet that deadline?**
  - ☐ **What was the end result?**

This question gives you a glimpse at how the applicant handles stress, as well as how they problem-solve. Did they dig in and get the necessary work done? This could indicate that they are determined and hardworking. Did they burn the midnight oil? This could mean they are a devoted, loyal employee who takes pride in their work. Did they go to a supervisor for help?

Maybe they didn't have faith in their ability, but at least they were self-aware and asked for help. Did they shrug their shoulders, come up short, and say they worked as fast as they could? This could mean the applicant is okay with mediocrity, lacks problem-solving skills, or just doesn't take pride in their job.

- **Tell me about a time when you went through a significant change in a short period of time.**
  - ☐ **How did you handle this change?**
  - ☐ **What was the end result?**

I like to ask this question when interviewing for openings at our transport company, because we are growing so quickly that change is a constant. We learn as we go, and the drivers have to be flexible. In addition, they must deal with last-minute changes on the road at times. Answers to this question can capture how well applicants adjust to such short-notice changes.

Remember not to lead applicants toward a particular answer. Leave it open-ended and let them tell you a story. Be a good listener, take notes, smile, and nod your head. If you look like you're enjoying what an applicant is saying, they will share more with you.

You should put together about four scenario-based questions. Remember to be clear when you explain the question, stating that you want to hear about a particular time, and not just how they would handle such a situation if it came up.

You may find that you have to reiterate your request. This can also be worth noting. How well does the applicant listen and follow directions? If you have to keep redirecting them, that can be an indication of a weakness as an employee.

The next questions are general, and if they do not apply to your company, you don't have to ask them, but try to incorporate as many as possible into your interview.

1. On a scale from one to ten, one being the least, and ten being the most, where would you rank your organizational level?

2. On a scale from one to ten, one being the least, and ten being the most, where would you rank your speed? Where would you rank your accuracy?

3. Why do you want to work here, and what is it about this company that interests you?

4. What other companies have you applied to work for in the last month?

5. On your last performance evaluation, in what two areas were you ranked the highest?

6. On your last performance evaluation, what one area needed the most improvement?

7. When we contact your former manager to verify your employment, what will he or she tell me about your last performance review?

Here are some of the responses you may look for:

Question 1: On a scale from one to ten, one being the least, and ten being the most, where would you rank your organizational level?

Office work can be a nightmare if you're not organized. But being *too* organized can also affect productivity. We have begun asking this question to our potential drivers as well as office employees, because drivers are responsible for cleaning their vans in their downtime. An applicant being organized can reflect on how much pride they might take in the appearance of their van.

Question 2: On a scale from one to ten, one being the least, and ten being the most, where would you rank your speed? Where would you rank your accuracy?

It is highly unlikely for anyone to rate a ten in both speed and accuracy. If an applicant answers ten for both, they are not being honest.

What to look for in answers to this question varies, depending on the position you are trying to fill. For example, the software we use at our billing company features "scrubber" technology, so if an employee forgets to complete a field or enters invalid data, the software instantaneously sends that entry into a queue for correction. So a data-entry worker who does a large volume with reasonable accuracy is more efficient than an extremely accurate but slow worker. The computer checking the work is much faster than any manual checking process.

If I am hiring a data-entry clerk, an applicant who rates an eight or better in speed with accuracy at seven or above would be preferred over someone who is a nine or ten in accuracy but a five in speed. This question is helpful when interviewing for production-based positions.

Question 3: Why do you want to work here, and what is it about this company that interests you?

This gives an applicant an opportunity to tell you if they researched your company. They may share what they can contribute to your company, or you can learn what their interests are, what job duties are most appealing to them, or where they see themselves at your company.

Question 4: What other companies have you applied to work for in the last month?

This will tell you how serious an applicant is about their job search. Are they blasting out resumes to any company with an opening? This could mean they are committed to finding a job. It could also mean they don't really know their professional interests.

You don't want to waste your time hiring someone who will hop to another job before long. If an applicant has applied to just a few companies, were their applications all for similar jobs? This could mean the applicant is a person who knows what they want and has narrowed their focus to jobs that will make them happy. But it might mean they are simply testing the waters to see what is out there and may not be committed to finding a job.

Use their answer as a starting point for more pressing questions if you are not clear on why they applied where they did. This is an interview, after all. It is your opportunity to get answers to questions you consider relevant.

Question 5: On your last performance evaluation, in what two areas were you ranked the highest?

Applicants love this question. Faces light up and they brag about their standout skills. Many employees do not receive regular evaluations, and that is fine. Go ahead and ask them to evaluate themselves. While you can't put too much weight on responses to this question, especially if applicants are rating themselves, it is helpful to know what a person thinks are their strengths and to see how they handle themselves when answering. Do they appear confident in their answer? Humble perhaps?

Question 6: On your last performance evaluation, what one area needed the most improvement?

Here is an opportunity to challenge applicants. Some people have a knack for making negatives sound positive—a trait that is itself actually a positive. If they come up with a response to this question that is not really negative, that shows quick thinking and creativity.

Quite often people will say they cannot think of anything. This may mean they don't want to share prior negative feedback because it was so bad, or it may mean they think they are perfect. Whatever the reason, it's a mark against an applicant if they cannot come up with any response.

Question 7: When I call your references, what will they tell me about your performance?

This provides an enlightening comparison point when you actually make those calls. It also encourages honest responses to your questions. If applicants know you intend on contacting their references, they will be more up front.

WHICH WAY OUT?

At our old offices, an indoor hallway led from our suite to the parking lot. The entrance from the parking lot was a glass door framed on either side by large windows. On this particular day, the candidate was a nervous wreck. For the entire interview, she avoided eye contact, stuttered, and sweated profusely. My heart went out to her. This was clearly torture for her.

After what felt like an eternity of questions, I got up to walk her out. I stepped into the hallway and watched her leave, thanking her for her time. She was so flustered that she walked headfirst into one of the windows, thinking it was a door. Her head rebounded backward like a basketball on a backboard. She seemed completely disoriented, so I ran toward her, asking if she was okay. She regained her bearings and bee-lined it out the door before I could reach her. I was mortified for the poor thing. I'd love to say I offered her a job, but it was not a happy ending for her.

What's Next?

After all the questions, take a few minutes to give applicants a quick rundown of your company. At this point, you want to make sure they feel as if your business would be a good fit for them. Tell them about your expectations, any uniform requirements, hours, benefits, and wages. Bring up anything that might be a deal breaker.

Give them the opportunity to ask questions. What an applicant asks can be instructive as well. Wanting to know about what their job duties would be or what skills they need are wonderful questions. These mean that the applicant wants to make sure they are a good fit for the job. If the only things they want to know about are benefits, paid days off, vacation time, and pay, this might mean they are only concerned about what they get out of the job, rather than what they can contribute to your company. Beware of the "me" attitude. This type of person usually has a hard time being happy anywhere. Make a note of the types of questions applicants ask for your reference.

If the applicant asks questions about the starting pay, discuss it promptly, so you don't advance to the next step with someone who may not be able to work for the wages offered. This discussion can be initially awkward. But once you've had this conversation multiple times with different applicants, you will become more comfortable navigating the topic. You never want an applicant to feel undervalued, but you must be honest if you cannot meet their expectations.

It is helpful to be aware of the going rate for the position you are hiring for. You can usually find out this information from a temp agency. These firms are typically up-to-date on reasonable wages for both employees with experience and workers new to a given line of work.

A sense of industry standards for pay is a helpful negotiation tool. Another tool for negotiating pay is this: Propose that a new hire start somewhere between their desired wage and the wage you have in mind. If they are confident in their ability, you can offer to raise their pay after they produce at a certain level. They can earn the wage they want if they are as good as they claim to be.

If the applicant is truly confident in their ability, they will go for this type of deal. If they hesitate, perhaps they aren't as good as they led you to believe. If you do offer up these types of deals and you end up hiring, be sure to follow through. All effective leaders know you are only as good as your word.

Once the interview process is done, tell them you will be in touch pending your decision to move forward with a hands-on test. Hands-on tests can be time-consuming, so save that for your finalists. Remember, your goal is to make hiring as easy and efficient as possible.

LICK, SLURP, CRUNCH

I will always remember a particular interview we conducted in one of our early years in business. A pleasant, middle-aged woman came in for an interview. At that time, my husband and I usually conducted interviews together, and as you will see in chapter 7, these early meetings were long, usually lasting about an hour.

We offered applicants water or coffee in an attempt to make them comfortable. We would hold the interviews in our break room, furnished with a basic table and chairs and little else. We did have a small box of Tootsie Pops on the table for our employees, in case they needed a little afternoon sugar rush.

The applicant declined water or coffee, but about five minutes into the interview, she excitedly announced that she would love to have a Tootsie Pop. My husband smiled and told her to go for it. For half an hour, she sucked on the lollipop and answered questions around aggressive licks and slurps. She twirled the candy around in her mouth and would yank it out with a resounding pop to answer a question.

Finally, she bit into the sucker with all her might, and blue candy crumbles dropped all over the table and onto her lap. She kept crunching away on the Tootsie Roll center, picking up dropped pieces and popping them in her mouth.

My husband and I ignored her strange table manners as best we could. Once the interview was complete, the woman stood up and vigorously shook our hands, thanking us for the sucker and walking out with the biggest smile on her face. I was glad we could make her day with a Tootsie Pop, sometimes it's best to just go with the flow, and then make yourself a reminder note in the file (*enjoyed a Tootsie Pop*).

5

FINAL INTERVIEW—DOES THIS APPLICANT KICK BUTT?

You are down to the final few applicants. Hopefully, you only have two or three in this round. Now what do you do with them? You already know you like them and feel they would be a good fit on your team, but now you need to confirm they have the skills they claimed to possess.

I hate to break it to you, but not everyone is 100 percent honest. This reality brings us to the hands-on portion of the interview. What you do at this interview will vary, based on the position and your needs. For any basic office job that requires computer work, I highly recommend (at the very least) a typing and ten-key test, as well as some basic Microsoft tests.

Here are some of the websites I use to test applicants. For typing speed, try one-minute typing tests at 10 Fast Fingers (http://10fastfingers.com/typing-test/english). This website lists words, rather than providing the tester with a sample paragraph. When typing a paragraph, the test taker can memorize a sentence and won't have to look at the screen the whole time, making it easier for them to get away with peeking at the keyboard. But a list of unrelated words forces test takers to look at the screen, and this type of assessment can more accurately reflect their ability.

Once the test is complete, the site displays the words per minute (wpm), number of keystrokes, how many words were typed correctly and incorrectly, and my favorite info, a percentage ranking comparing the tester to all other people who have taken the same test on this site.

For ten-key speed, I use 10 Key Tutor (http://www.10keytutor.com/). Most ten-key tests online are fairly similar. I have always used this one, but I don't think it has any special advantages.

For Microsoft software proficiency, I have applicants take the tests at ProProfs (http://www.proprofs.com/quiz-school/topic/office-software). This website tests familiarity with Microsoft Office software, including Access, Excel, Office, Outlook, PowerPoint, and Word. It tests for basic knowledge with a fairly broad variety of questions. The site produces a certificate at the end showing the test taker's percentage of correct answers.

For critical thinking and problem-solving tests, I like the tests available from Psychology Today (https://www.psychologytoday.com/tests). My favorite, by far, is the Analytical Reasoning Test. It is a one-hour test that challenges an applicant's problem-solving skills, critical thinking, logic, and more.

I use this test for potential dispatchers at our transport company, because they need to be able to handle phone calls with customers who are ill and often impatient, manage dispatch calls coming in, change schedules on the fly, and fill in future schedules like puzzle pieces. This test does cost $10 (which it doesn't tell you until you click to get the results), but if you have only a few applicants, it is well worth the expense.

Ask an experienced and effective staffer already working in the position you're filling to take the test and use their results as a guideline to find people with a similar skill set. If you are looking for someone to complement a current employee's skills, you can still use the test as a reference to fill in the gaps.

These are just a few sites I like to use. You can find tests online that will allow you to evaluate your applicants' knowledge in virtually any area. You can even create your own tests based on real-life scenarios that applicants may encounter with your company.

It may seem unnecessary to have an applicant who claims a typing speed of 45 wpm take a typing test. But you would be amazed by the results I've seen. Potential hires sit down in front of the computer and don't know proper finger placement, make a ton of mistakes, or test at half the speed that their certificate states. I actually asked some of our externs about their struggles with typing. They told me their school gave them the same paragraph to type, over and over, until they reached 35 wpm. Many told me they had simply memorized the paragraph to increase their speed. Put a typist like that in front of a list of words, and you are lucky to get 20 wpm out of them. Anyone can talk a good game, so I always tell people I want to see the skill.

FANCY FINGERS

Because the majority of the jobs at our billing company are nearly 100 percent computer work, we always have applicants take a typing test, and in general, we expect decent typing and ten-key skills. We ask applicants their typing speed and whether they have a certificate. About half of the candidates have certificates. Certified or not, all finalists must sit at a computer and show us their skills.

One woman told us she loved working on computers and was a very good typist and ten-keyed really well, although she didn't know her exact speed. She thought she was around 40 wpm. So we sat her down at the computer and pulled up the typing test. She began typing with two fingers. Literally. She put her two index fingers out and started typing away. She was not bad for only using two fingers. She hit about 30 wpm, but she had to look at her hands to hit the right keys, which obviously slowed her down. Usually we prefer our employees to type at least 45 to 50 wpm, but I was impressed at the speed she accomplished.

In the back of my mind, I thought maybe her ten-key is fabulous. So we set her up on the ten-key test and off she went, typing across the top row of the keyboard. She used the same two fingers and buzzed across the top numbers. She was surprisingly faster at the numbers than she was at regular typing. Out of curiosity, I asked her if she could use the ten-key pad, because we use calculators frequently. She looked at me quizzically, and I pointed to the ten-key pad on the keyboard. She laughed and shook her head. But she goes down in my book as the fastest two-finger typist in town.

6

REFERENCE CHECK—SMOOTH SAILING OR STORM COMING?

The final step should go smoothly, if you did well in choosing your top candidates. That said, always be ready for a surprise when you check references.

Let me start this section with another story. My husband is a great judge of character. He has a master's degree in criminal justice and volunteered alongside a parole officer at a local prison for years. He completed interrogation classes and has a natural knack for reading people.

The interview for one applicant started off a little rough. I could tell my husband was not connecting with the candidate right out of the gate. He was very cold toward the interviewee, and I was ready for him to rush through the interview.

But once we picked up momentum, the applicant proved quite likable. The man was fabulous through all the follow-up interviews—a people person and flexible on his shifts. We expected he would join our team.

But when we called his references, we didn't get any responses. Once the background check came back, it showed a multitude of felonies, some as recent as five years earlier. Because of the nature of some of our contracts, and because we deal with disabled and elderly clients, we cannot consider applicants with felonies for that position. We learned something important that day: Always go with your initial gut feeling, and in this case, my husband's instincts at first were right on target.

When contacting references, you should attempt to contact three people who have worked alongside your applicant and can attest to their abilities and skills. Make the candidate aware that you plan to contact their references. You should always perform your checks on the phone, rather than through email so you can hear their tone of voice. Make sure you check your state's guidelines on what questions can be legally asked. Assuming you have the flexibility to ask any questions, here is our recommended list:

1. What dates did the applicant work for you?

2. What were the applicant's title and job duties?

3. If the applicant were to reapply for that position, would they be considered for rehiring and why?

4. What was the reason for their separation from your company?

5. Was the applicant punctual and reliable?

6. How did the applicant get along with their peers and supervisors?

7. What were the applicant's two strongest assets?

8. What was one thing the applicant needed to improve on?

9. Is there anything else you can tell me about the applicant?

Your main goal in asking these questions is verifying what the candidate has already told you. Some are the same questions you asked during the interview process. This overlap is intentional, to give you an idea of how truthful the applicant was during the interview process and expand your sense of their performance in previous positions. Compare the reference's responses to the candidate's answers and make sure they are similar. If they do not match up, this should be a red flag.

If your state limits what questions you can ask previous employers, you may need to get more creative. Go ahead and contact them to confirm what is allowed, usually hire and separation dates, and then consider others who may provide a trustworthy reference. A parent or spouse will not likely be the best fit. Consider a pastor or minister, people from the candidate's church, or past coworkers or supervisors who have also moved on to other companies.

Once you have found an applicant whose references satisfy you, you are ready to move forward with background checks, drug screens, and any other final pre-employment processes necessary before completing your new hire.

NO COMPUTERS, PLEASE

When you walk into our main office, you are greeted by rows of cubicles, each one holding a computer workstation. Our ads usually state that applicants should be comfortable working on computers and have proficient typing skills. We bring the applicants in through the main office into a back room.

One memorable candidate came through the office and sat down to begin her interview. I asked her about her favorite part of previous jobs, and she repeatedly responded with answers like "helping customers" or "talking to people." She said over and over that she was such a social person. Every time I would ask her to name a least favorite part about a job, she would go on and on about how much she hated working on computers. She thought computers were so boring, and they made the day go slowly.

I remember thinking through the entire interview, *You did see all the computers when you walked through the office, right?* Mind-boggling. Needless to say, she was not a good fit for the position.

7

EXPLORE OTHER INTERVIEW FORMATS AND LEARN FROM OUR MISTAKES

As I mentioned at the beginning of the book, we have used a multitude of different interview processes in staffing our business. We took pieces from each interview method to develop the process I just shared with you. Our system is efficient, successful, and quite easy, once you learn it well. In this chapter, I will review the other processes we used and explain what we did and did not like about each.

Our first process was for a small billing company, and we had plenty of time to find qualified employees. Our ad was extremely basic, specifying only the job position and wage. During the interview process, we asked a lot of the same questions, although the specific wordings have changed as we gained experience. The biggest difference in the process was that we called every person in to meet face-to-face, and in a single session, we would ask all the questions we now ask over the length of two interviews (by phone and in person). This usually took a solid hour, and sometimes longer if the applicant was a talker. Then we would sit them at a computer and have them take a typing test.

The good: The extended in-person interview allowed us to spend a lot of time with the applicants. By the time we got to the end of an hour with someone, they were usually opening up and telling us a lot. We learned generous amounts of information from these candidates. If your goal is to put someone at ease so they will open up, a longer interview may work.

The bad: In California, we are required to ask the exact same questions of all applicants, for the sake of fairness. Even if we quickly lost interest in an applicant after a few questions, we still had to complete the interview. We also realized having each person perform the typing test was pointless if we were not seriously considering them for the position. What a waste of time. As the saying goes, time is money.

Our next process was a slight modification of the first interview format. Our ad was still basic, but we decided to do two interviews rather than one. We split our questions into two sets, similar to what we use now. We called all the applicants in for the first round, which usually lasted about thirty to forty-five minutes. If we liked an applicant, we would set them up for a second interview.

The second portion lasted about ten minutes, and then they would perform the hands-on portion after the questions. We modified our hands-on portion to include both a typing test and an exam I made to test basic billing knowledge. Applicants had to answer two pages of questions using coding books and basic math skills.

The good: Compared to our first process, this shortened the length of time spent on first interviews. The increased hands-on portion was enlightening. It showed who had a true knowledge and who falsely claimed skills they did not have.

The bad: People would have to come to our office a second time for a super-short interview. We were not sure what such a minimal meeting accomplished, since we had already met them face-to-face once before.

We implemented our third process at the recommendation of a business coach. It was a group interview process. We also modified our ads, similar to the ads we now use, including more detail so people better understood what we were looking for. In the ad, we asked the applicants to call a Google number by a certain date. When they called the number, a recording asked them to specify three reasons why they thought they would be the best fit for the job. They had three minutes to list and explain those reasons. We listened to the voice-mails and narrowed the pool down to the top six to ten people, depending on how many candidates we needed to hire. With this group interview process, assessing more than ten applicants can be highly time-consuming.

The guidelines for arrival at the interview were strict, and at the listed time, the door was locked and no late arrivals were allowed to enter. The group interview began with the interviewees introducing themselves, and then we introduced our company. We proceeded to a round-robin question-and-answer session, where each candidate had an opportunity to answer the same question. There was a large variety of questions, many similar to the ones we have listed in this book. At the end of the interview, which lasted two to two and a half hours, we would tell the applicants that we would contact the chosen finalists. At that point, if we chose to do a hands-on portion, we would call them in individually.

The good: This application process eliminated a lot of the lazy applicants. Calling a Google number and explaining why they should be considered for an interview was more work than some job seekers were willing to do. This also allowed us to hear the applicant on the phone and determine whether they spoke clearly, could think under pressure, and followed directions well. Overall, it was efficient. Little time went into the process, and it was easy to compare applicants' answers when they were all sitting in front of us, answering the same questions.

The bad: Because fewer people applied, our pool of applicants dramatically shrank. In the group interview, candidates can feed off their peers' answers. You do have an opportunity to see who can think for themselves, but some applicants' answers were likely negatively affected by nerves and the pressure of being surrounded by competitors. Depending on the position you are hiring for, this group situation can be a plus or a minus.

THE RESEARCHER

We had a driver opening at our transport company, and I had identified a promising candidate in the first round. On the phone, she came off as a positive, upbeat person with a sense of humor, potentially delightful company for our passengers. So I called her in for a face-to-face interview. She took a seat in the office and we began.

As I was asking questions, I felt a little confused by some of her answers. It seemed I was missing something, but I couldn't quite put my finger on it. She kept saying things like, "I don't really like working with customers," and "I love to type and talk on the phone." Once I asked her what aspect of this job appealed to her the most, the answer hit me like a ton of bricks. She said she would be a great fit for our *billing* company because she loves the medical field.

She was interviewing for the wrong company. Both of our businesses are located at the same physical location, and she had researched the wrong one online. So even though the ad was for a driver, she thought the position was in data entry. She came in to sell me on how great she was at computer work, when I was hiring for an outgoing person who worked well with customers. Thumbs up to her for researching before the interview, but unfortunately, she missed the mark.

8

KEEPING IT LEGAL

Every state has different laws governing hiring and employment, and you'll need to do your homework for your area. But I do want to use this section to reiterate some basic interviewing guidelines that you should keep in mind to comply with federal laws. I am not an attorney, nor do I advise on the law, but it is important to research relevant rules and follow guidelines to protect your company and yourself.

Applicants frequently share plenty of information that potential employers are not allowed to ask about, but it is still important to understand that you can't ask for certain information, including age, conviction records, disabilities, marital or family status, national origin/race, religion, sex, height/weight, or citizenship.

This is not an exhaustive list, and there are exceptions to these rules. For example, if someone is applying to work in a bar, they must be of minimum age, and you are able to ask if they meet that requirement. If someone is applying to work in the medical field and cannot appear on the Office of Inspector General list, you can confirm that they are not on the list. Use care in how you word your questions, and be sure that the questions you are asking pertain to the job duty the applicant is applying for.

You can find more details on basic federal employment policy through the Equal Employment Opportunity Commission (https://www.eeoc.gov/laws/practices/).

You must ask the same questions of all applicants (but do check with your state's requirements). This is to protect you. By completing the same interview with all candidates, you ensure that applicants cannot claim unfair treatment. Be sure to go through the same exact set of questions in its entirety with all applicants.

Make sure all notes taken during the interview process are factual and objective. Write down exactly what they say and avoid writing down opinions or personal notes. All resumes and written notes from an interview should be retained. File them or scan them as a record, should you ever need to produce them.

Staffing an HR person is a luxury for most small businesses, so you'll likely want to give yourself a crash course in relevant regulations and know when they change. After all, ignorance is not an excuse for breaking the law. There are companies that specialize in third-party HR services in our area. They offer the convenience of having an HR employee on staff, for a fraction of the cost.

We send our HR partners an email when we need something, and they get back to us in a timely fashion. They built our employee handbooks for us and advise us on topics ranging from changing laws, to how to properly release employees from a position while protecting ourselves as the employer.

If you have not already looked into a solution like this in your area, I would recommend doing a quick search for third-party HR companies. They can make your life a little easier.

WHAT JUST HAPPENED?

I received a phone call from an applicant for a driver position. She asked if she could drop off her resume. I told her I preferred that she fax or email it to me, or submit it via a job search site, which is where she said she had found our ad. I told her I would review her information and let her know if I would like to conduct a preliminary phone interview.

Over the course of the next few hours, I received multiple voice-mails from the same woman, insisting that she would much rather drop off her resume in person. I chose to avoid responding, as I had already recommended multiple options for submission.

I was in the break room making my lunch when I spotted a girl with vibrant pink and purple hair wandering around outside the window. After about five minutes of walking back and forth, she knocked on our office door. It turns out this was the young lady who wanted to drop off her resume. Mind you, I was just about to sit down and enjoy my lunch.

The wild-haired visitor told our office staff that she wanted to give me her resume. They kindly pointed me out through the break room window, so I stuck my head out the door. I reached for the paper and quickly thanked her, saying that I will get back to her soon. Her reply: Seeing as she was here already, she wanted to go ahead and do an interview. I told her I usually conduct first-round interviews on the phone, and I would be happy to call her later to schedule something.

She literally began begging me to please, please do it now, since she had come all this way just to meet me. I glanced back at my lunch, quickly growing cold, and agreed to do a short interview. I took her to the back room, printed out a question list, and proceeded.

She told me her least favorite part of working at the discount store was that it was really hard remembering where all the items went, and sometimes they would have more than two people in their checkout line, which was stressful and caused her to make mistakes. I was not digging this interview at all when she stopped me to ask whether the position was full-time or part-time. I informed—or rather, reminded—her that the ad stated this was a full-time position.

She literally jumped out of the chair announcing, "Oh, I only want a part-time job, never mind!" With that, she swung the door open and high-tailed it out of the office, leaving me to consume my (cold) lunch in peace. Mental note: be more protective of my time. Stick with your process, and make others conform.

9

HIRE POWER

As you have seen, the questions, how you ask them, and the setting you ask them in all impact the responses you get from applicants. Remember, the ultimate goal is to keep your interviewees relaxed, build a trust with them, find a common link, and do your best to get them to open up to you. As you have seen in some of the stories in the book, people will tell you some amazing things once they are comfortable.

Your job as the interviewer is to simply ask the questions and listen well. Allow applicants to answer fully, and don't interrupt them unless they have wandered off track. You can prompt them, but allow them to elaborate, tell stories, and carry the conversation. This way they can sell you on their abilities, or dig their own grave. Nod your head, smile, and look completely enthralled in what they are telling you, even if you are not.

You may have to re-ask a question occasionally because the applicant failed to answer it. Sometimes they truly misunderstood the question, and other times they try to redirect intentionally. Either way, give them a second opportunity. If they still fail to answer the question, make a note. This could be a sign they do not follow directions well or are simply not good at communicating.

Remember to give the applicant a rundown of your company, any included benefits, your expectations, and your company culture, but not too early in the interview. Make sure you have completed all your questions first, so that you know they are answering the questions honestly and not saying what they think you want to hear. Less is more until the questioning is complete.

The next and final step: Get out there and hire some amazing new employees.

Make the Offer

Once we decide who we want to hire, we call them right away. Don't allow extra time for them to find a job somewhere else. When I call our top candidate, I tell them they are our first choice and ask if they would like to join our team. In most instances, as long as you have been speedy with the process, they will usually say yes.

What should you do if they turn it down? Well, that is why you call the first choice before calling the ones you are passing up. Assuming you liked any of the other finalists, you can still call them and offer them the job in the same manner. They don't need to know they were second on the list.

Once you have a new team member, allow a day or two before calling the others to let them know the position has been filled—in case your new hire changes their mind after sleeping on it. It has happened to us more than once. When you do finally call runners-up, let them know you liked them, and ask if you can keep their resumes on file for future openings. It doesn't hurt to keep the door open, and it will save you some work in the near future if they are still looking for a job when you have another position available.

YOU CAN'T BEAT EXPERIENCE

I was interviewing for the driver position and upon asking the applicant what made her a good fit for the job, she told me she really enjoyed driving and had a knack for it. She continued on about how she was really good at following directions and had a lot of experience driving.

I didn't recall seeing any driving experience on her resume, so I asked her when and where she had obtained the driving experience. Her response, "Oh, well, I've been driving a long time. I used to steal my mom's car a lot when I was real young and so I got a lot of driving experience way before I even had a license. So I have been driving a long time. I am real good at it."

Well, there you go. I guess there is nothing like experience.

❧

Congratulations, you now know how to run the most efficient interviewing process ever.

We believe that our system is the most efficient way to interview potential employees. At the very least, you can save yourself time and headaches by learning from our extensive trial and error. If you use this process, you will find it efficient and effective, but only after some practice. The more you use the system, the more comfortable you will become with each step. Applicants will pick up on your level of comfort. Just as you are trying to read them, they are observing you. Take a breath, have a good time, and above all else, trust your instincts. They are usually right in the end.

ABOUT THE AUTHOR

Amy Wolf founded her first business, a medical billing company, in 2002 near Sacramento, California. What began as a side job in her master bedroom blossomed into a full-fledged business within six months, resulting in the need to expand into a building and hire employees.

She earned a degree in business and accounting from Sacramento State.

Being in the medical field for so many years made her realize there was a great need for a reliable medical transportation company in their area. Amy and her husband, Jacob, decided to fill the void and birthed their second business, a company that successfully re-created the nonemergency medical transportation industry in their area and blew their competition away. They built the business to eight vehicles and over fifteen employees in one year.

Amy continues to grow and manage both companies, enjoys helping others find success and happiness, and loves being a wife, mother of two, and author. Follow Amy Wolf on Facebook: https://www.facebook.com/amyjwolfwrites/.